THE BOYS' HOME INDU SCHOOL

From Euston Road to Chalk Farm

by Gillian Gear

On Tuesday, 24 November 1857, a meeting took place at 186 Fleet Street that was to be crucial in the setting up of a special school for destitute, unconvicted boys. This meeting was the idea of two friends, both called George Bell, but unrelated.

The first George was the eldest son of Matthew Bell, a stationer and bookbinder of Richmond in the North Riding of Yorkshire. He was born in October 1814 and became a prominent publisher. After his marriage in 1840 he lived over his Fleet Street offices until 1849, when he left for 2 Haverstock Terrace (now 28 Belsize Grove). Then in 1860 he moved to a house nearby with four acres, which he called 'Westcroft', leased from Eton College. In 1882 the Eton Estate sold it for redevelopment and George moved on to Hampstead Hill Gardens, where he lived until his death in 1890.

George was a friend of Dr Harvey Goodwin, a Fellow and mathematical lecturer at Caius College, Cambridge, who was later to become the Bishop of Carlisle. As well as his London offices, George had a publishing business in Cambridge which produced mathematical works for Goodwin. There, in 1852/4, Harvey Goodwin, with colleagues and friends, had been involved in the setting up of an industrial school for boys, which he believed formed the basis for the London school later set up by the Bells. Goodwin considered himself to be the 'grandfather' of the London school.

The second Bell, George William, was born in November 1822 in Aldersgate Street, London, the son of a merchant, William Bell. The family business, Bell Brothers & Company, had financial difficulties in 1842 (although they obtained discharge from their creditors in 1845) and this forced George to find employment. Though qualified as a barrister, he entered the insurance business and in 1858 he was the chief clerk, later secretary, to the Law Fire Insurance Society. George William lived at his father's house, 36 Woburn Place, Bloomsbury, until 1860, when he married. At first he took a house in nearby Bernard Street but in 1863 he and his family moved to St Edmund's Terrace (also called St John's Terrace), Primrose Hill and again in 1889 to 7 Albert Road, where he lived until his death in 1910.

It was while George William was walking to the house of his friend, George Bell, near Haverstock Hill in Hampstead, that the idea was formed for setting up a special school.

George William also had connections with special children's homes. His brother, Frederick Hayley Bell, was the paid secretary of an association set up to help the children and wives of soldiers serving in the Crimean War. Towards the end of the war the Soldiers' Daughters' Home was established in Hampstead and George William's sister, Leonora, was to supervise its running, while George William himself was appointed secretary. The matron of the Home was a soldier's wife, Mrs Hannah Rayment.

At the 1857 meeting in Fleet Street, George read a paper describing the five existing London reformatories for convicted destitute boys as being generally successful. He felt, however, that there was a need for homes for unconvicted destitute children. It was his aim to open a home where boys would be kept clean, clothed, fed, taught and put under control, without the influence of bad example.[1]

Founders, staff and boys at the Regent's Park Road site, c1880. The Bells are in the front row: George, second from right, and George William, third from right.

Engravings from The Story of the Boys' Home, *c1900. Above, stacking wood, and below, the central premises at Chalk Farm.*

George's friends included Christian Socialists and members of the Pre-Raphaelite movement, for whom his publishing company produced the *Oxford and Cambridge Magazine* as well as other works. They decided to form a committee with George Bell as honorary secretary, and the Rev. F.D. Maurice, Thomas Hughes (author of *Tom Brown's Schooldays*) and George Bell were appointed as trustees. Both Maurice and Hughes also helped to found the Working Men's College.

A house was rented at 44 Euston Road, which opened on the 26 February 1858 as an industrial school. In June of the same year it received its government certificate under the Industrial Schools Act of 1857, the first London school to do so. The founders were obviously aware of other similar schools set up by philanthropists, for the minutes of the meeting held on 8 December recorded that letters were sent to Mary Carpenter, Matthew Davenport and Mr Baker, amongst other leading pioneers of the reformatory and industrial school movement.

Sergeant Ebenezer Rayment, the husband of the matron of the Soldiers' Daughters' Home, started work as the master on 25 February 1858 and his wife joined him on 18 July as matron - this family was to have a long connection with the Home. After Ebenezer's death in 1871, his widow continued as matron, with her son George as the master. Later another son, Henry, was to act as secretary to the school.

The need to raise money was a major priority for the group. Each member of the committee was urged to collect a specific contribution before the Christmas of 1858. Hughes agreed to write to *The*

The Boys' Home Industrial School in Regent's Park Road c.1904. (Courtesy of Roger Cline)

Both these boys were sent through refuges but the others who joined them were recommended by individuals - clergymen, police, law court officials - concerned about the welfare of particular children. Later, with the establishment of the London School Board, many children were sent by that body and subsequently by the London County Council.

According to the first annual report, the boys first cleaned the house and then began to learn needlework, presumably to provide themselves with reasonable clothing. A mast and poles were set up outside for climbing, and sawing and chopping firewood was begun. Other skills such as carpentry, tailoring, and shoemaking were taught by tradesmen. Some

Times, asking for donations from the general public, and in March 1859 a Thomas Station was appointed as a paid assistant secretary and collector.

Troublesome boys
At first, just two boys, aged 13, were taken in. One, sent by the master of the Grotto Passage Refuge, had been living on the streets but was considered to be an industrious boy, keen to work but uneducated. His father was dead, his mother had remarried and had a second family, and they were extremely poor. The step-father ill-treated the boy and forced him to lead a vagabond life. Troublesome at first, this boy settled down in a few months and four years later he joined the Royal Navy.

The other boy was the son of a widow who worked as a washerwoman and had one other son. His attendance at a ragged school had been irregular and he had been dismissed from the shoe-black brigade for dishonesty and disobedience. He ran away from the Boys' Home (having persuaded three other boys to escape with him) but was brought back after eight days' absence. Eighteen months later, he was still at the Home and, despite occasional trouble, the master described him as affectionate and greatly improved, bright and intelligent looking, and he appeared to work industriously.

The Band of the Boys' Home (foreground) forms part of the Guard of Honour to King Edward VII at the opening of UCS, Frognal, 1907. They are in the uniform of the 1st Cadet Battalion Royal Fusiliers, City of London, to which they were attached.

Boys working in the bakery at the Home in Regent's Park Road c.1904. (Courtesy of Roger Cline.)

of the better behaved children were sent out to local houses for short periods to work but this was frequently the cause of problems.

Part of the day was spent in schoolwork: the boys were taught reading, writing, arithmetic, singing, geography and object lessons. Saturday was a half holiday and on Sunday there was church, with classes from 9am to 10am and 3pm to 4pm.

Within its first year more space was needed and the house next door was rented. The Home then held fifty boys. Most of those listed in the 1861 Census had been born in the London area but one boy was born in China and another in India, suggesting that their fathers were in the services. One other boy had been born in Norfolk, another in Hampshire and two in Ireland.

Move to Chalk Farm
In 1865, the Midland Railway needed the site in Euston Road to enlarge their St Pancras station and the school moved to some unfinished buildings near to Chalk Farm station in Regent's Park Road. The property, part of which can still be seen at the corner with King Henry's Road, was made up of three unfinished houses and a yard, which were taken on a ninety-nine year lease from the governors of Eton College. These premises were smaller than those in Euston Road, which meant that twelve of the boys had to be transferred to other schools at York, Manchester and Liverpool, but a further house was bought in 1866 with money given by Lady Truro. With the school and the workshops, which were later built, 100 boys could be admitted, and in 1885 further new buildings were added.

The boys slept in separate houses, each accommodating about 25, and there was a bed for each boy - a rare thing for members of poor families. Each room had a monitor and each house a master or matron who lived in, to act as parent to the boys. They were instructed to: 'guide them, no less by action than by firm discipline, to establish a happy family feeling and to attract their once ragged and disorderly pupils by the force of kindly teaching and good example'.[2]

When the Boys' Home moved to Regent's Park Road, there had been no room for them in neighbouring churches and so services were held in the schoolroom, which local people also attended. When the area became built up, an iron church was erected in Ainger Road, which took over part of the parish of St Saviour, Eton Road. The chaplain, the Rev. C.J. Fuller, ran services with the help of other clergy and afterwards members of the congregation could visit the Home to see the boys tucking in to their Sunday dinner.

A site for a permanent church was given by Eton College and, in 1872, St Mary's Primrose Hill was opened, which the boys attended with the Rev. Fuller as school chaplain and vicar until 1889. After that time the school and the parish church seem to have gone their separate ways and the Truro Room was built and used as a church.

The Home settled down to a routine of trade, work and schoolwork in fairly equal balance. One of the trades taught was tailoring. Initially this appears to have been done entirely by hand but in 1890 the Home reported the acquisition of a sewing machine. The tailors' shop was thus described:

'In the midst of the boys....little boys who are stitching away merrily, like elves in the fairy tale. At one end, on the regular tailor's board, the master tailor sits cross-legged, after the manner of tailors, while several youths, cross-legged also on the same shopboard, represent the skilled element in the workshop. Below these elder ones, stand and sit the rest of the elves, who are patching, piecing, darning, sewing on buttons and stitching up rents. These tailor boys, with ordinary good conduct, will be able to make a living for themselves anywhere. The boys, indeed, cannot all be tailors but they all will attain sufficient skill to patch and repair their own clothes and that is an accomplishment, which still stands them in good stead in any part of the world in which they may be thrown.[3]

George Bell's interest was reflected in the trade of printing, an unusual one for industrial schools. The boys produced their own magazine and other material for themselves, and also provided a useful income by doing work for outside customers, including other schools.

Many of the boys were taught to play musical instruments with a view to their finding employment in military bands when they left the Home. It was felt that the chances of a boy succeeding in the services were greater if he went in with the trade of a bandsman. The school band, under Mr Brookes, played for local garden parties and school treats.

The Pre-Raphaelite connection
Some boys were described as cabinet-makers and carpenters, and appear to have produced very high

Off to Seaside Camp, from the Annual Report, 1914.

quality work, which illustrates the links with the Pre-Raphaelite group. In fact, some of the boys went to work for the William Morris Company when they left the school and when, in 1860, Burne-Jones married Georgiana Macdonald, the boys made a table, black high-backed chairs with rush seats and a black wood panelled sofa from designs by Philip Webb as wedding presents. They also made a walnut pedestal writing desk, which was inscribed and presented to the secretary of the Reformatory and Refuge Union, Arthur Maddison, and some 'choice bits of furniture' for the home of William Bell. A rocking horse made for the grandchildren of Edward Bell is on display at the Bethnal Green Museum of Childhood. The school also sold a range of items of furniture to the general public.

One lucrative source of income for the Home was the selling of firewood to local householders, using timber imported from Sweden and brought up on the Regent's Canal by barge. On 25 July 1877, the boys were resting while offloading timber from a barge at Ice Well Wharf, St Pancras, when one fell into the water: the master, George Underwood, jumped overboard and saved the boy's life. By 1890, the sale of firewood was decreasing and it was subsequently dropped altogether as it was not considered good training for the boys.

When George Bell died in 1890 he left a gift of £60 to form the nucleus of a founder's prize, and George William provided a silver watch and chain as the first prize. Founders' Day was held in June each year - a time when many of the old boys revisited the Home. At that time the management committee was very large, having 24 members, and there was also a guild of lady visitors with 18 members. In 1911, the honorary secretary, R.H. Glanfield, was called before a Departmental Committee established to look into the running of reformatory and industrial schools. In his evidence Glanfield, who was also on the executive council of the Refuge and Reformatory Union and of the Children's Aid Society, described how the Home had 134 boys from the age of seven upwards, and that the largest number was sent by the London County Council.

The boys spent two hours a day in recreation, which included cricket and football (pitches were hired in Regent's Park) and a reading room used in the winter for such things as draughts and chess; gymnastics were taught by an ex-soldier. He estimated that 75% of the boys were moderately good swimmers, despite the school having no pool of its own. They did, however, have a miniature rifle range and a playground and cloister under the dining hall for recreation where, at the time, the current craze was whip top. One of the reasons behind the encouragement of sport was to help the boys to develop healthily, and once a year they were measured to check their growth. The doctor called quarterly to inspect them and they were also visited by an optician and a dentist. On the whole, illnesses were dealt with in the hospital wing at the Home, but for operations the boys were sent to the Temperance Hospital in Hampstead Road.

The school was inspected by representatives of the Home Office and the LCC. Sometimes the amount of grant received depended on the standard achieved. There were three levels, and the Boys' Home was frequently assessed at the highest of them.

By 1916 there seem to have been some difficulties in obtaining an effective management committee. Edward Bell, George's son, was asked if he and his brother would join the committee, which was described as being in a 'very reduced state'. This may have influenced the decision to close the Home down in 1920, when the government directed that new buildings should be found in the country or it would withdraw its certificate and therefore its financial support. The children were either transferred to other schools or were found jobs.

As well as the Boys' Home in Regent's Park Road, there was a small school for girls, run by Mrs G.W. Bell, in Charlotte Street, and an auxiliary Home for working boys in St George's Square. An associated farm school was established in East Barnet in 1860 by Lt. Col. W.J. Gillum, who had married Leonora Bell.

The Boys' Home helped over 1,000 destitute boys over sixty years. Although the surviving records are limited, they appear to show a well run home, strict but not unduly harsh for its period, and one that provided a good standard of education and care that the boys could not possibly have expected otherwise.

In the words of one of the old boys, who had emigrated to Brisbane: 'Parted some thousands of miles from the old Home, I like to hear about it and often I think of the old days, some of the happy days of my life spent there, and I think if any Old Boy has reason to be grateful I have. I remember that I went to that school in Euston Road a poor sickly boy, without father, mother, sister or brother or friends in the wide world, and I never knew a mother's love till I went there.'[4]

Notes
1 Notes on facsimile of original Certificate of the Boys' Home.
2 Walford, Edward, *Old and New London*, Vol V p297.
3 *The Story of the Boys' Home*, p3, printed at the Boys' Home c1900.
4 *Ibid*, p20.

Sources
I should like to record my thanks to Miss Glanville (great-granddaughter of George Bell) for allowing me access to family records.
A list of other sources is available on request.

Further Reading
Beck, Gladys, 'A Service Bright & Brief', *Camden History Review* 2.

THE ROYAL MAIL AND RAILWAY CARRIAGE WORKS

Coach builders in St Pancras

by David Honour

The year 1835 was an important one in the story of the Royal Mail Coach. Since 1784 all the Royal Mail Coaches had been built in a factory on Millbank Row, Westminster, owned by members of the Vidler family. In 1835 the family lost their contract to build the coaches and in that same year they were built for the first time in Gough Street, St Pancras.

Background

Two years after the first successful Mail Coach had run from Bristol to London in 1784, John Palmer, whose idea it had been and who had become Comptroller General of the Post Office, was looking for a more dependable coach to perform the service. In 1786, John Besant, who described himself as an Engineer, patented a coach design that met with Palmer's enthusiastic approval and which was immediately adopted by the Post Office as their standard Mail Coach. John Palmer had found his dependable vehicle and it became known as the 'Patent Mail Coach'.

John Besant died unexpectedly in 1791, aged 46, and his partner John Vidler immediately took over the business, which he continued from their manufactory on Millbank Row. The Vidler family subsequently held a series of 14-year contracts to build the coaches and, during the years up to 1835, their coach evolved into the vehicle that helped to engender the 'Romance' of the Mail Coach.

In 1835 events, driven by Government pressure to obtain the best value for money in all its areas of responsibility, made it inevitable that the contract for Mail Coaches would be put out to tender. From the first there had been no competition of any sort for the contract to supply them, but a series of

Joseph Wright's Mail Coach, modelled by one of his employees, Thomas Wilson.

House of Commons Select Committee reports, ending in 1835, advised that the coaches could be got cheaper and that things must change. Finch Vidler, son of the first John Vidler, had come to over-estimate his family's own importance to the Post Office, and had seriously misjudged the strength of his negotiating position. His awkward behaviour ensured that he eventually found himself banned from tendering for the contract at all. The Post Office, too, in barring Vidler found themselves in a difficult position for at the start of 1836 they would have no Mail Coaches at all to run the service.

England, Scotland and Wales had been divided into three areas, and advertisements in July 1835 sought tenders for the supply of Mail Coaches for these districts. The successful companies were Croal & Wallace for the Northern District and Wright & Horne and Williams for the Midland and Southern Districts. The new contractors did not let the Post Office down for, by building more than one new coach per day in the last months of 1835, around 250 Mail Coaches were ready for service in January 1836.

The St Pancras Connection
The St Pancras connection is through Joseph Wright and William Horne, who were partners in the largest stage-coach building company in London. William Horne was the brother of Benjamin Worthy Horne, an innkeeper and coaching contractor, who was later a partner in the well-known Victorian transport company Chaplin & Horne. William Horne had been Joseph Wright's partner for only three or four years when they won the Mail Coach contract in 1835. Wright had started as an apprentice in 1808, became a partner in 1820, and by degrees had taken over the company from the original partners, one of whom was his father-in-law, James Bigg Wright.

The company, originally known as Wright & Powell, had begun trading in Ray Street, Clerkenwell, just before 1808, and may itself have descended from an even earlier company of coach builders. They had swiftly become the largest stage-coach builders in London, being described as such in 1811 in a House of Commons Report. Around 1813 they extended their business with premises in Great New Street in the City, and in 1822/23 additional buildings were acquired in Castle Street, Clerkenwell, including an adjoining property in Turnmill Street.

At the beginning of August 1835, Wright & Horne, who had formed an association with a coach-builder based in Bristol called Walter Williams (who had independently made enquiries of the Post Office about the work), were sure that the Mail Coach contract was theirs, though as yet unsigned. It was then that the problems of 'success' began to make themselves apparent. Wright & Horne (and Joseph Wright in particular) were not going to let go of existing business to make the Mail Coach and so they had to expand. They found additional factory space in Gough Street, St Pancras, off Gray's Inn Road, at the southern end of Lord Calthorpe's estate.

The Gough Street Site
Though there had been farms and other buildings on the Calthorpe Estate before 1800, a private Act of Parliament was promoted to facilitate the development of the estate for building purposes. There was a coach factory on the estate from before 1803, which is shown in a plan of the parish by John Thompson. This factory, owned by John Leader from at least 1799, can be seen running eastwards from the then Gray's Inn Lane, in two sections divided by a road. The rear portion is approximately where the later coach factory came to stand on the east side of Gough Street.

By 1812, the estate was being laid out in a planned development. The portion of this first manufactory fronting on to Gray's Inn Lane now lay under what was to be the south side of Calthorpe Street and the 'new' Blue Lion Yard. A builder/developer, Nathaniel Stallwood, took a lease on this site in 1815, and in his hands the building of (Upper) Calthorpe Street continued through the 1820s. A 'new intended street', Gough Street, was also laid out and the site of the easterly portion of the original manufactory was redeveloped. A new factory was constructed to a very particular plan, and the site was let on the 1st July 1812 to James Collingridge, Thomas Rowley and George Mansell, a company of coachbuilders.

Part of Thompson's map of St Pancras parish, c1800, showing a coach factory on the Calthorpe Estate.

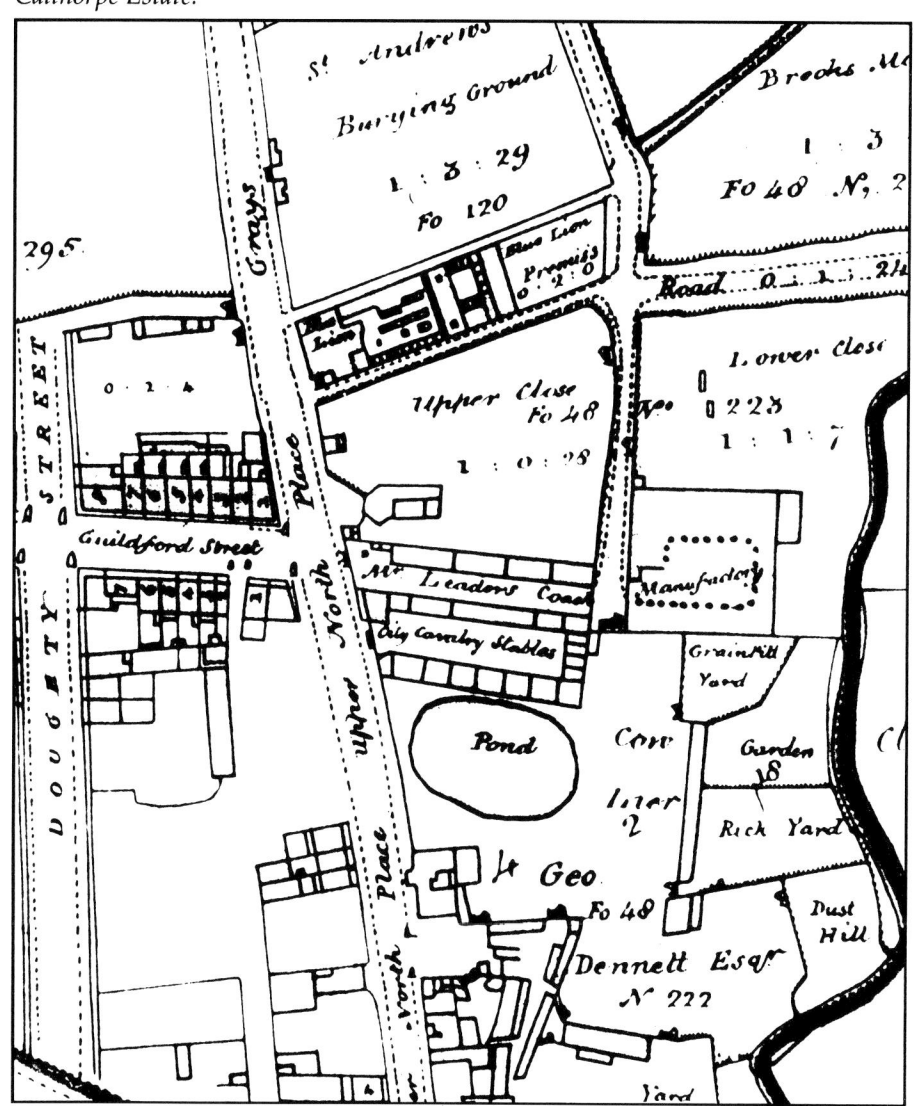

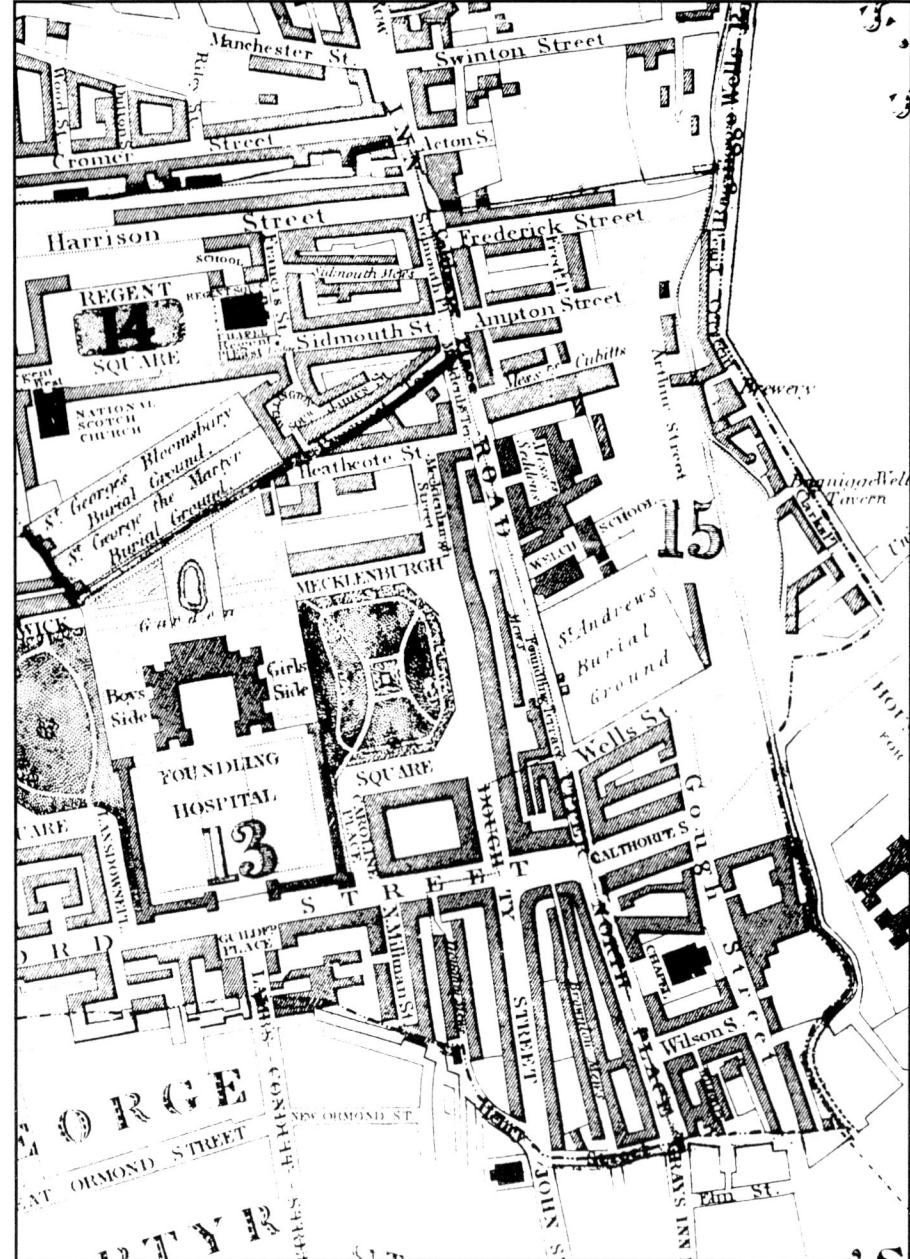

The Calthorpe Street area in Greenwood's parish map of St Pancras, 1834.

Joseph Wright and his wife, Elizabeth.

The Greenwood parish map of 1834 (reproduced above) shows that Calthorpe Street had been laid out to run eastwards from Gray's Inn Lane, with Gough Street crossing it at right-angles. The eastern portion of Calthorpe Street took a line towards the north side of the Middlesex House of Correction across the River Fleet. The new manufactory, which was 70 feet down the southern part of the 'new' street, backed on to the river, which ran southwards from Bagnigge Wells and on down to the Thames. The manufactory had an impressive one-storey, brick building fronting on to Gough Street with a central double gateway which led through this into a yard surrounded on the other three sides by wooden sheds. Opposite the entrance was the manager's office, brick-built with two rooms and a toilet. This was the layout of the site when Wright & Horne took it over in an agreement dated 31st October 1835.

An Indenture dated 24th December 1835 assigned the factory to William Chaplin and it is evident that this was the security for a loan made to Wright & Horne. Setting up the Mail Coach business was extremely expensive and a great deal of initial investment was required. William Chaplin was a prominent stage and mail coach contractor whose base was the Swan with Two Necks in Lad Lane in the City. Later, in November 1837, Chaplin bought Horne's quarter share in the site from Joseph Wright. Chaplin was a very astute businessman, eventually becoming a director of the London South Western Railway, and would only have invested in a sound business.

North of the manufactory lay a long triangle of land which, before the development of Calthorpe Street, was used as a sort of garden ground. Joseph Wright added this to the factory site in September 1836 and it was quickly covered with buildings.

The Joseph Wright Residences
The last piece of the jigsaw of the manufactory complex was put into place when Joseph Wright decided to build his family house next door. This house, the lease of which ran from September 1839, was the first to be built in Lower Calthorpe Street. Now No. 26 Calthorpe Street, it is the only part of the factory buildings to survive.

The style of this substantial brick-built, five storeyed, corner house is rather like those built by Nathaniel Stallwood on the earlier part of Calthorpe Street, save for the fact that the ground floor is covered in rusticated stucco (it is of course possible that it was built by Stallwood, who lived in Calthorpe Street). If one visited the house and then took a short walk eastwards across the King's Cross Road to Lloyd Baker Street, one could judge the rise of Joseph Wright's fortunes, for there, at No. 43 Lloyd Baker Street, is the little house that Wright lived in when he first became a partner in the business. The difference in size is instructive.

The 26 Calthorpe Street house remained Joseph Wright's home from 1839 until 1857, by which time he had effectively retired from the day-to-day running of his businesses. He is a man who has dropped out of history, but a list of some of his business interests and achievements might colour in the life of what is now a very dilapidated house.

Later Achievements
From Calthorpe Street Joseph Wright ran the largest stage-coach building firm in London and was responsible for most of the Victorian First Class Mail coaches (including the Mail Coach now in the Science Museum). He built omnibuses and in this and other factories he made railway coaches for all the great railway companies. In the 1840s he was for a time coaching superintendent for the London & Greenwich Railway. From 1841 he held the same position with the London & Birmingham Railway and later with the Southern Division of the London North Western Railway. In 1842 he patented an early version of a railway bogie carriage. He built the London & Birmingham Railway's first Royal Coach and the Queen Adelaide Coach (which still survives in York). The London General Omnibus Company appointed him a judge in their competition for designs for a standard London Bus and he subsequently became their bus surveyor. If you step over the threshold of a modern tube or main line railway coach and see 'Metro Cammell', that company is descended in part from Wright's business. It is a breathtaking list and it is not complete, but this summary suggests something of the achievements of the man whose home this was.

In 1845 Joseph Wright and his sons founded a new railway carriage factory at Saltley in Birmingham. The stage-coach and Mail Coach were beginning to be made irrelevant by the spread of railways. The Mail Coach contract was cancelled in 1848 and most of Wright's London factories had been closed by the time the Gough Street coach manufactory closed in 1852. He kept the various leases, sublet the properties, including Gough Street, and used the income to augment his growing fortune. By an arrangement that would be frowned upon today and was then, even though he was in full time employment as the coaching superintendent of the London & Birmingham Railway and subsequently the London North Western Railway, he supplied his own department with coaches built in his own factories as an independent contractor. The London & Birmingham Railway had sacked Edward Bury, who supplied their engines and was in exactly the same business position, and yet for some reason they ignored Joseph Wright.

Wright was a clever man with tremendous energy, which he used to create a great company, and it was a huge shock to those who knew him when he was accidentally gassed to death in his sleep in November 1859, the night before a visit to the Birmingham works. He was genuinely mourned by his workers.

In 1994 the poor condition of No. 26 Calthorpe Street, with bushes sprouting from its structure, makes it difficult to imagine the young Queen Victoria climbing into the Royal Carriage built in the factory behind; and, with thoughts of the Royal Mail Coaches speeding through the countryside, it is surely ironic that, by one of those strange turns of history, the site of the Royal Mail and Railway Carriage Works is now occupied by part of the Royal Mail.

Sources of Information
(details from the Author)
Post Office Archives, Greater London Record Office, Public Record Office, Birmingham Reference Library, Patent Office, House of Lords Records Office.

No. 26 Calthorpe Street, the Wrights' family home.

Nos. 45, 44 and 43 Lloyd Baker Street. Wright's earlier house, No. 43, is the corner property.

A BELSIZE MAP OF 1762

by Roy Allen

The map shown here, by kind permission of Guildhall Library, is dated 1762 and entitled 'A Plan of an Estate situate at Hampsted in ye County of Middlesex'. Some twenty acres in extent, the estate is part of the Manor of Belsize, held by the Dean and Chapter of Westminster. In modern terms the property runs north-eastwards from half-way up Daleham Mews, soon joining Belsize Lane; it would now include Belsize Crescent, Lyndhurst Gardens (except the top) and most of Wedderburn Road, with an exten-

The Belsize Map of 1762 (by courtesy of the Guildhall Library, City of London)

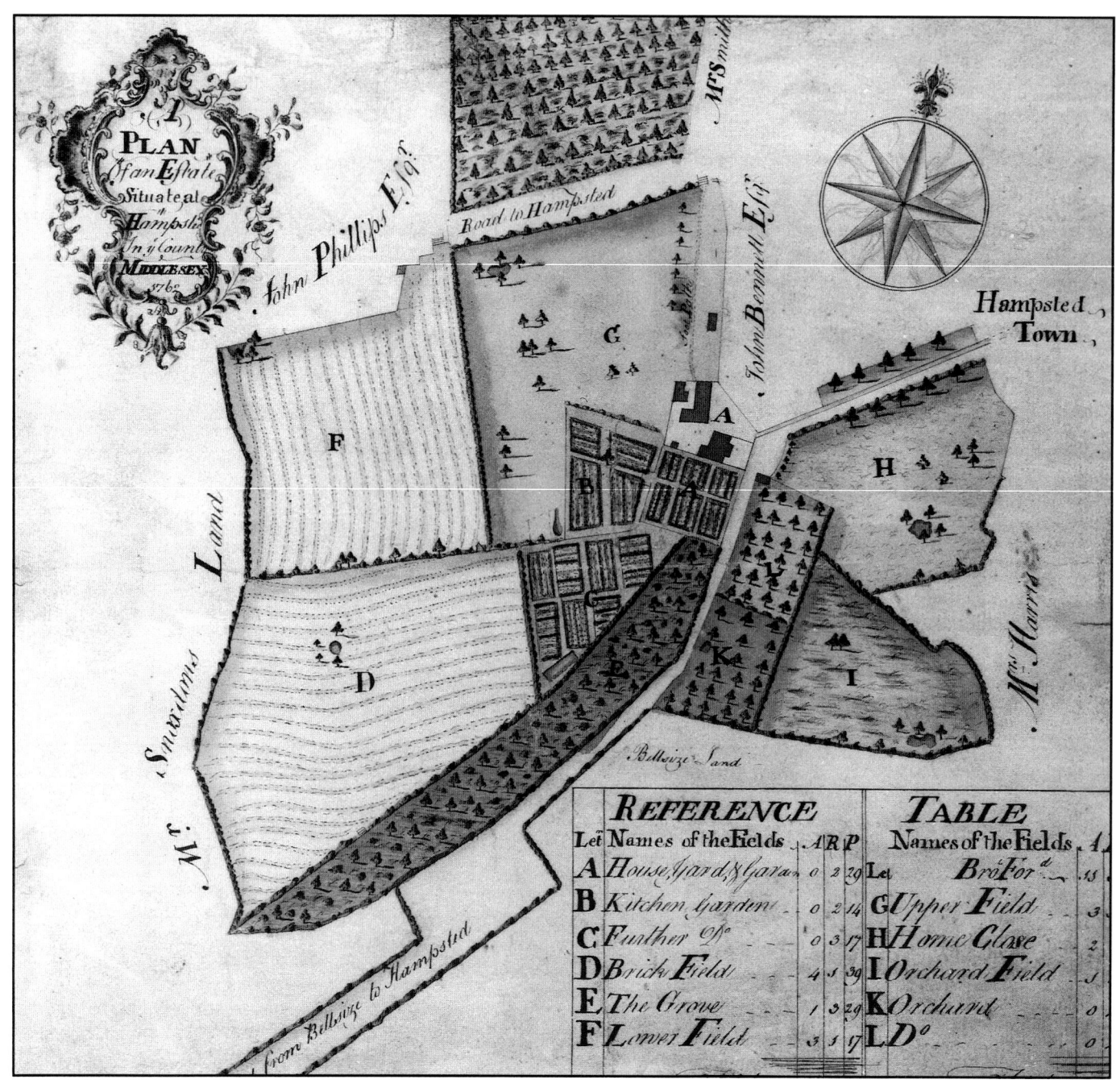

sion around Hunters Lodge on the opposite side of the lane.

Mostly in green tints, this is a decorative map, the more so because liberties are taken with outlying features: thus 'Hampsted Town' is placed at the start of Belsize Lane, thereby helping to make the layout more compact. The wood or orchard at the top is not part of the estate and is not on earlier maps; it looks like an embellishment, filling the space between the cartouche and the compass-rose.

At nearly thirty-three inches to the mile (the scale is in chains) detail such as ponds and field gates can be shown. The surveyor does not identify himself but he can hardly be the James Ellis who in the same year made the large Hampstead map: he would have known that the neighbour to the west was Edward Snoxell (a farmer), not Snoxdon.

The main road, Haverstock Hill and Rosslyn Hill, could have been inserted across the top right corner but it would upset the balance of the map. 'Road to Hampsted' is therefore a tree-lined backwater, perhaps already known as The Grove (the map also has a wood of that name) and once the drive to what became Rosslyn House. This is not marked but was near the cartouche; the occupant, shown as Phillips, might in fact be Fellowes (see CHS *Newsletter* 124). One name can be confirmed: there has been a Harris on Haverstock Hill for over eighty years.

We are not told who (if anyone) occupied the main dwelling (marked **A** on the map), probably still the White House of John Grove's manorial survey of 1714. George Todd, a Baltic merchant, arrived in 1803 and he demolished the place in 1811, having built nearby the villa that was finally known as Belsize Court. The map shows the original course of Belsize Lane, before Todd diverted the middle part eastwards to the far side of the two orchards (**K** and **L**), and into land on either side, thus creating the sharp bend at Hunters Lodge (CHS *Newsletter* 128).

Field boundaries compare reasonably well with those of 1714 and 1679 (William Gent's manorial survey) but names are volatile. Thus

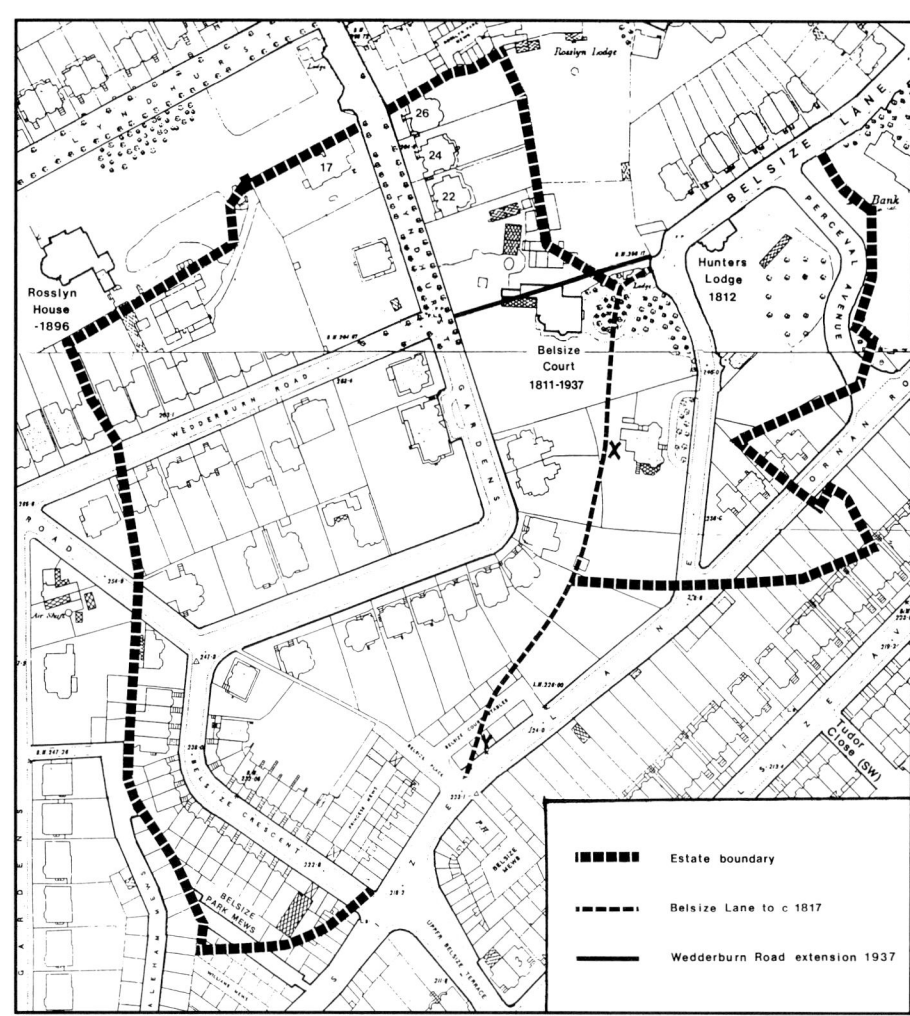

Composite plan of the same estate, based on OS maps of 1893 (top) and 1916 (bottom). Between X and Y the old Belsize Lane became an ornamental walk, marked by the OS on their 1866 map. Part of the boundary east of the modern lane has been modified in the light of 1866 landmarks. West of the lane, the north-east corner of the estate survives in garden walls at 17, 26, 24 and 22 Lyndhurst Gardens.

Lower Field (**F**, top left) was *Haley's Picle* in 1714, the tenant in 1679 having been Thomas Haley; picle is a variant of pightle, a small field. Haley knew the enclosure as *Conduit Field*, presumably because it was on the way to Shepherd's Well (not marked but near the margin to the left of the date).

Only *Brick Field* (**D**, in bottom left; originally **D+C**) kept its name throughout the period. Professor F.M.L. Thompson suggests, on p8 of his *Hampstead: Building a Borough* (1974), that this is where 400,000 bricks were produced under a contract of 1496, probably for an early version of Belsize House.

These two fields are on the edge of the Manor of Belsize, the land to the west being in that of Hampstead. To the right of the 'S' in Snoxdon there is a kink in the boundary; this may be seen near the top of Daleham Mews, in the garden wall at the back of 25 Belsize Crescent. The reverse kink further down is visible to the right of 11 Belsize Park Mews, high up.

What prompted the survey is not known. Failure to name an occupant suggests that the house was empty, as it was in 1714; perhaps the map was commissioned for showing to prospective tenants. In any case it usefully covers part of an area left blank on Ellis's map, which depicts only the eastern half of the Manor of Belsize.

CULTURAL FINDS IN FINCHLEY ROAD

by Susan Palmer

During her researches for the Finchley Road section of our latest publication The Streets of West Hampstead, *the author unearthed a surprising amount of information about the road's cultural interests at the turn of the century.*

1. ARTISTS' STUDIOS

It is hard now, as one stands in the grimy and fume-laden Finchley Road to imagine that it was, in the nineteenth century, a place where artists chose to set up their studios. This article is about just such an artist and a family of sculptors and a stained glass artist whose spacious, one might even say palatial, purpose-designed studios were featured in the architectural press on their completion.

Henry John Yeend King

Henry John Yeend King, more usually known as Yeend King, was a successful and prolific landscape and rustic genre painter. Born in London in 1855, the son of Henry King, he studied in Paris and exhibited at the Royal Academy for the first time in 1876, thereafter exhibiting one or more pictures there virtually every year until 1924, the year of his death. He also exhibited at a number of other galleries in Britain and abroad, including in Berlin, Munich and Chicago, winning the bronze medal at the 1889 *Exposition Universelle* in Paris. He was elected RBA (member of the Royal Society of British Artists, Suffolk Street) in 1879; RI (member of the Royal Institute of Painters in Watercolours) in 1886, later becoming a Vice President; and he was also a member of the Royal Institute of Painters in Oil Colours. In 1898 his picture *Milking Time* was bought by the Tate Gallery for the Chantrey Bequest. His works may be seen in the Tate, the Walker Art Gallery and in the Reading, Rochdale and Sheffield galleries. Abroad his *The garden near the river* is in the Sydney Museum. Christoper Wood describes him[1] 'as a typical late Victorian painter of rustic genre, often garden scenes with pretty girls', but notes that 'his robust plein air technique and bold colours reflect his Paris training'. This may well explain the comparatively high prices his work has been fetching on the market in recent years. *The Mill Stream* and *News from Abroad* were estimated at

Architect's drawing for Yeend King's studio in Finchley Road, from The Building News, *5 May 1893. (British Architectural Library, RIBA, London)*

£2,500-£3,000 at Phillips of Toronto and Sothebys respectively in 1992, and in 1993 his *At the Farm Gate* and *Young Fishermen* were estimated at £8,000-£12,000 and £6,000-£8,000 respectively at Sothebys.

From 1876 to 1892 Yeend King lived at various addresses in St John's Wood. It was in 1893 that he moved to 103 Finchley Road, to one of the large houses later swept away in the development of the Hilgrove Estate. By now very successful, he proceeded to add a large studio to the house. Whilst in the course of building this was illustrated by a full-page spread in *The Building News* for 5 May 1893 (see accompanying illustration). The studio measured 25 feet by 28 feet internally. Across its east end ran a minstrels' gallery, which formed a passage from the main house to a smaller studio built above the model's rooms, which was used for painting small work. There was also a 10 foot square glass-house for painting outdoor subjects. Clearly the building of this studio was not accomplished without some protest from the neighbours, as the writer of the article comments '[the glass-house] is placed immediately opposite the large studio light which is formed in the roof, no side light being provided owing to certain ideas of the adjoining owner'. The architect was Frederick J. Lewis of 263 Strand, and the builders Messrs. Myring and Co. of 69 Abbey Road, St John's Wood.

Yeend King remained at 103 Finchley Road with its extensive studio complex until 1908 when he moved to 139 Alexandra Road. In 1911 he moved to Maida Vale where he died in 1924.

His daughter, Lilian (later Mrs Hatton Fraenkl), was also an artist. She was born in Paris in 1882 and would have been eleven when the family moved to Finchley Road. No doubt she would have watched her father at work in his studio there. It was from her father's house at 219 Maida Vale that she exhibited at the Royal Academy in 1919 and 1921. Later known as a landscape painter, this artist's two early works exhibited at the Royal Academy were family portraits: *The artist's mother* and *Eustace, son of H. Yeend King Esq.*

Yeend King's obituary in *The Times* of 12 June 1924 paints an engaging picture of this one time resident of Finchley Road: 'In appearance Yeend King was a contrast to the conventional idea of an artist, being clean-shaven, wearing his hair short, and having a genial smile and a great fund of humour. Like most painters, however, he was a real Bohemian, with a wonderful collection of funny stories, which he told well. He was seldom without a snuff box, although he himself was not a constant snuff-taker.... His loss will be deeply felt, not only by his brother-artists but by a great number of friends in every walk of life.'

The Forsyth Family
Further up the Finchley Road, Number 325 was, from 1882 to c.1905, home to a family whose members included two sculptors and an artist in stained glass. James Forsyth (1826-1910) and James Nesfield Forsyth, his son (d.1942), were sculptors of considerable repute. James' works were mainly of the monumental order, with some portrait busts, whereas James Nesfield specialised in busts and sepulchral works. They exhibited at the Royal Academy from 1864-1889 and 1885-1927 respectively. In 1879 James Forsyth, then living at 23 Baker Street, had a new studio built in Finchley Road. Variously described in the early years as 'The Studios, Finchley Road' and 'The Studio, Finchley New Road', it adjoined the Finchley Road station of the LNWR at Number 325 (and possibly also 327, but this is unclear). [As a guide to today's pedestrian, O'Henery's public house is Number 317, and the house immediately to the south of The Hampstead Bible School of Faith Number 337]. *The Builder* for 17 May 1879 records with some excitement the opening of these new premises on 1 May 1879. They are described as 'appear[ing] in every way fitted for the execution and display, on a large scale, of his art works', and as being in 'such a good position' and 'so large and convenient'. They consisted of a dwelling house of four floors, flanked by a gallery 43 feet long. This gallery led, through a modelling room 27 feet high, to the shops for carvers, masons, pointers and joiners, with a yard in the centre spanned by a travelling crane equal to 20 tons. The architect was W. Smith of John Street, Adelphi, and the builders Messrs Patman and Fotheringham. Sadly, the article omitted to include any illustrations of these extensive premises.

James Nesfield Forsyth exhibited at the Royal Academy from 325 Finchley Road from 1885. He remained at this address until 1905/6, when he moved to '1 Studio' 335 Finchley Road, evidently another complex of studios further up the road. He left Finchley Road in 1913/14, moving first to Church Row Studios, Heath Street. In 1921 he is listed as exhibiting at the Royal Academy 'c/o 57 Abbey Road', St John's Wood, and in 1924 and 1927 he exhibited, for the last time at the Royal Academy, from 18 Lymington Road.

Several works by both father and son can be seen in public buildings in London and around the country. James Forsyth was responsible for *Christus Consolator* at the Missionary College, Mill Hill; *The Wicked Servant*, one of a series illustrating the biblical parables in Frome Church; *St Paul Preaching at Athens* in alabaster for the pulpit in Worcester Cathedral and a statuette of the late Earl of Dudley in the Shire Hall, Worcester. Sadly, also by him is a memorial to his three year old daughter Agnes, who died in 1864, in Abney Park Cemetery. Standing on the perimeter road between the two gates, it takes the form of 'a coped Gothic tabernacle with a moving portrait medallion in high relief'.[2] Abroad, his *Andromeda* can be seen in the Sydney Museum. James Nesfield Forsyth executed medallions of the poet, William Cowper, and of 'The author of Elia' for Lower Edmonton Church; a recumbent effigy of the Very Rev. Gilbert Elliot, Dean, for Bristol Cathedral and a marble statue of the late Bishop of Wakefield, Dr Walsham How, for Wakefield Cathedral. He was also responsible for two busts of local residents: a terracotta bust of William Wallford, FRCS, who was living at the time (1889) in 'Dunelm', Number 120 on the east side of Finchley Road; and a bronze bust of the architect, Professor Banister Fletcher (Senior), then living at 21 Woodchurch Road, and whose monument is in Hampstead Cemetery (see page 14).

The third member of the Forsyth triumvirate was John Dudley Forsyth (d.1926), a stained glass painter. He was presumably also a son of James Forsyth, but of this no proof has been found. He is first listed as exhibiting at the Royal Academy in 1896, when his address is given as 'The Studios, Finchley Road'. He left Number 325 sometime between 1904 and 1907 when he reappears at 51 Broadhurst Gardens. By this date he describes himself on his Royal Academy submissions as 'Architect', but the works he exhibited at the Royal Academy exhibitions until 1925, the year before his death, are, without exception, designs for stained glass.[3] These included a competition design for the Lord Strathcona memorial window, Westminster Abbey; a design for a stained glass memorial panel presented to Stanhope Forbes

R.A. by the Architectural Association; a design for a stained glass window in the Italian staircase, Finsbury Circus House; a stained glass window designed for the Council Chamber, County Hall, London, and a design for a proposed nave window in St Paul's Cathedral. One of his windows can be seen in the south aisle of Westminster Abbey, but sadly, his 'unusual windows', including a dome window[4], in the Baltic Exchange, City of London, will no doubt have been destroyed by the recent bomb. Closer to home, one of the apses in the cemetery chapels at the Hampstead Cemetery contains three windows designed by J. Dudley Forsyth.

1. *The Dictionary of Victorian Painters*, Antique Collectors' Club, 1978.

2. Chris Brooks in *Mortal Remains: The History and Present State of the Victorian and Edwardian Cemetery*, Wheaton with the Victorian Society, 1989.

3. Nor is he listed in *Directory of British Architects 1834-1900*, Mansell, 1993, compiled from the papers held in the British Architectural Library of the Royal Institute of British Architects.

4. *A Guide to Stained Glass in Britain*, Painton Cowen, 1985.

2. JAMES HAYSMAN AND THE INTERNATIONAL COLLEGE

339 Finchley Road, on the corner of Lymington Road, which now houses The Hampstead Bible School of Faith and two shops selling reproduction fireplaces and futons, is a building which looks very much (see p. 16) as if it has seen better days. This article will attempt to show something of those better days, and of the vision of one man and the international system of education which he devised.

This imposing red brick building (see the contemporary illustration), the International College designed by Banister Fletcher the elder, was built in 1885 for James Haysman, A.C.P., F.R.G.S., F.[R].S.A., an educationalist who had already founded a series of schools elsewhere in London. It was opened on 16 July 1885 by the Marquis of Lorne, and *The Architect* of 24 July 1885 took the opportunity to give an enthusiastic description of the building. The style was described as 'a free adaptation of the Gothic', and it was said to have 'both externally and internally a light, cheerful and airy appearance which [could] not fail to be appreciated by master and pupils'. The scale

Design by Banister Fletcher (Senior) for the International College in Finchley Road (not Highgate, as stated), from The Building News, *7 August 1885. On the right is the top of Lymington Road. (Camden's Local Studies Library)*

of the building, and indeed of the school it housed, can probably best be appreciated by enumerating the detailed physical description of the interior given in *The Architect*. There were four floors, and a tower containing an astronomical observatory [which has clearly been demolished at some time since]. The first and second floors were devoted to living rooms and dormitories for the boarders and masters (it was built to accommodate about 100 boarders as well as an additional 100 day scholars). On the ground floor were several classrooms and a large hall seated for 800 persons, with an open pitch-pine roof and at one end a raised platform with an organ erected by Messrs. Chappell & Co. of Bond Street. The basement contained a dining hall, a large covered playground,

90 feet by 45 feet, and domestic offices. There was also a large open playground and a bathroom. One wonders how many of these features survive inside today.

Four years after the International College was opened, in May 1889, a public banquet was given in the Whitehall Rooms of the Hotel Metropole in celebration of the twenty-fifth anniversary of James Haysman's System of International Education and of the fiftieth birthday of the man who was now principal of The International College, Finchley Road, of the Anglo-French College in Burgess Park, off Finchley Road to the north, and of a similar college at Richmond. Before giving more details of the banquet, reported at great length in the *Hampstead and*

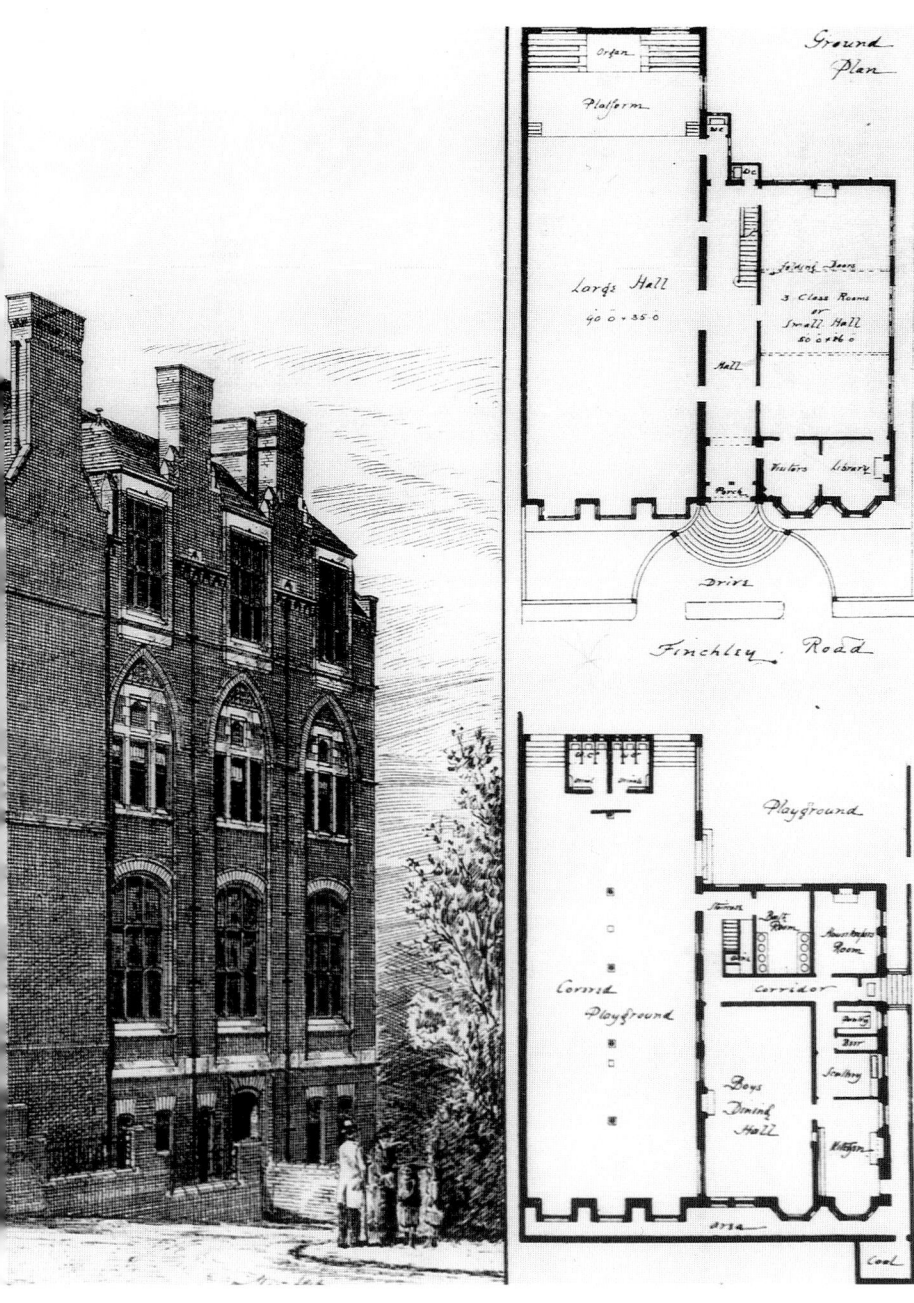

Highgate Express of 25 May 1889, it is worth pausing to examine the career of this indefatigable man.

Born in 1839, James Haysman began his career at the age of twelve in 1851 as a pupil-teacher at the school attached to Christ Church, Stepney. Having served as an apprentice there for five years from 1852 he was in 1857 appointed Assistant Master at the Endowed Schools, Isleworth. Then, having studied at St Mark's College for two years, at the end of 1860 he took charge of St Paul's School, Bow. The number of pupils increased rapidly, and in 1861, following an experiment that he had already made at Isleworth, he started evening classes for youths and adults, not only instructing them in the subjects essential to their business or professions, but offering additional classes in drawing, science, elocution and vocal music. 'Many of the students at those classes are now holding important and responsible positions in the borough of Mile End', comments the writer of the *Ham and High* article.

From 1862 he started taking in boarders, and in 1864 a large house of twenty seven rooms was erected near St Paul's Church. Three years later in 1865 the large hall of the East London College and two residences for masters were erected in Burdett Road, and by the end of the year the College had four hundred pupils. Great demand from middle class parents soon prompted the opening of a College for two hundred pupils at Hackney. Mindful too of the evening classes he had provided at St Paul's, Bow, he rented the Burdett Hall, Limehouse, for daily use as a lower division of the East London College. It rapidly became full, and another similar school was taken at High Street, Poplar. Then, listening again to parental pressure, he turned his attention to the education of girls, establishing in 1867 the Victoria College, Bow Road; the Alexandra College, Stainsby Road, Poplar, and a College in Victoria Park Road, Hackney. The girls at these schools were, he claimed in 1889, 'not one iota behind those attending the Girls' High Schools of today in intelligence, perseverance and ability'.

Fears of a cholera epidemic in 1867 led Mr Haysman to look for a large house in the suburbs as a possible refuge for his East End boarders. He found such premises in Burgess Park, just off Finchley Road, and opened them under the title of the Anglo-French College. Fears of cholera proved groundless and they were not needed for their original purpose, but they rapidly filled with pupils. He also moved his family here from Burdett Road, commuting every day to the East End to supervise all of his schools.

At this point, following what the *Ham and High* coyly refers to as 'an act of over confidence' disaster struck, and James Haysman was defrauded of the lease, premises and furniture of the East London College and one of its affiliated schools. Despite the conviction of the individual concerned at the Old Bailey in 1869 (he was incidentally sentenced to five years penal servitude), it was impossible to restore the smooth working of so extensive a system, and Haysman had also suffered a heavy pecuniary loss. Efforts were made to revive the schools, and a number of public meetings held, but in the end he leased the East London College premises in Burdett Road to the School Board for London as an industrial school. Twelve years later Dr Barnardo rented, and subsequently bought, the premises, renaming them Leopold House.

The Haysman International System
Meanwhile in 1869 James Haysman was free of most of his schools, and could devote his energies to realizing and perfecting his International System of Education, for which, by 1889, he was known and honoured worldwide, and which, as the *Ham and High* reporter put it 'has proved of incalculable value to thousands who were

The remains of No. 339 Finchley Road today.

Portrait of James Haysman, from the Hampstead and Highgate Express, 25 May 1889.

destined for a commercial life'. 'Such a system was first talked of forty years ago [i.e. c.1849], but it was not until Mr Haysman developed it and put into it some of the energy and enterprise of which he possesses such an abundant supply that it made any great mark in the educational world.' The leading features of the system were foreign languages, science and art. This may not seem very revolutionary to us today, but one must remember that at this date the great public schools were putting the emphasis mainly on Latin, Greek and mathematics. Mr Haysman contended that a thorough study of modern languages should be substituted for the dead languages Latin and Greek. Gradually a network of schools in France and Germany were affiliated on certain conditions with schools in London. Boys were sent to live abroad for short periods to perfect their knowledge of a foreign language, and one of the merits of the system was held to be that his pupils could pass from Mr Haysman's schools in London to those on the Continent and still be under the same conditions; there was abundant food, sound education and parental care, the same as under his own roof (and, incidentally, no corporal punishment).

In 1889, at the time of the public banquet, Mr Haysman was still full of ideas for the expansion of his system. The International College in Finchley Road, opened four years earlier, had, he said, been founded for his sons (he had a large family of sons and daughters) to serve as a Central Institution from which they might continue his work. He envisaged the advantages of the system being extended to daily pupils from all over London, affording them special facilities for spending, under proper supervision and at a moderate cost, a few months of each year at a French or German school, and returning each autumn to their parents and to their day school to perfect their English education and pass the necessary examinations. He had also founded at the Finchley Road College the North West London School of Art and Science, opened by Lord Knutsford, the Colonial Secretary, in 1888, and the North West London Vocal and Orchestral Society. He was also busy establishing there an Athenaeum, with which was to be combined a botanical, a geological and a literary society. Abroad, his thoughts were turning to Spain, as he revealed in his speech on the occasion of the banquet: 'His idea was that the commerce of Great Britain should be carried on by British youths, and not by imported Germans [this provoked applause]. He saw no reason why a youth of seventeen years of age should not know three languages, and be fitted to take a position as a Foreign Correspondence clerk. It was within the reach of every youth of that age to learn French, German and Spanish. He attached special importance to the last-mentioned. British trade with Spain had greatly increased of recent years, and the Argentine Republic was open to us. He had therefore decided to extend his system to Spain, and had selected Barcelona as the centre for carrying on the work......He also intended to open a kind of register, to which merchants might refer and select good and capable clerks from the pupils of the International College.'

The celebratory banquet would seem from the detailed report in the *Ham and High* to have been a typical late Victorian affair, with an imposing guest list, many laudatory speeches and toasts and much applause. Lighter moments were, however, insured : at intervals during the evening Madame Agnes Larckom and Mr Iver McKay sang several songs, and Mr Horner, a former pupil of Mr Haysman, recited 'in an admirable manner' *An old sailor's story*. In addition 'Mr W.H.Harper proved himself an admirable accompanist and tastefully and artistically rendered two pianoforte solos'. The evening concluded with the singing of *Auld Lang Syne*.

Locally as well as nationally and internationally the International College had a good reputation. It is interesting to note that an advertisement, thought to date from 1893, for 'very handsome, semi-detached residences' in Greencroft Gardens, specifies their proximity to 'Haysman's International School for Boys in Finchley Road', along with the various railway stations, the Hampstead Public Baths in Finchley Road, the Hampstead Conservatoire of Music in Eton Avenue and 'the High School for Girls adjacent to Fitzjohns Avenue' [South Hampstead High School; University College School did not move to Frognal from Gower Street until 1907].[5] Nevertheless the conclusion of this article is a sad one, for eighteen years later the International College and James Haysman's name disappear from Finchley Road between the 1907 and 1908 Post Office Directories. By then he will have been sixty nine and will no doubt have wished to retire. Perhaps his sons did not wish to continue his work as he had hoped. One day we may find more evidence of this remarkable man and his work, and be able to put a proper conclusion to the story.

5 Camden Local History Collection, Swiss Cottage Library, Accession No. M.5390.

A TALE OF HOFMANN AND BROOKE

Local links with science-based industry

by David H. Leaback

Though very different in origins, background and training, August Wilhelm Hofmann (1818-1892) and Edward Brooke (1831-1892) were both sometime residents of Camden, and their lives were strangely linked in a story that illustrates persistent British attitudes to science, technology and industry.[1]

Hofmann was born, raised and educated in the small Prussian town of Giessen. He entered the University there, first to read philosophy and languages, but he was later drawn to study chemistry under Justus Liebig. The latter was earning an impressive international reputation, not only for the important advances in organic chemistry taking place in his laboratory, but also for the influential ideas he was promulgating in his widely read books. Liebig had brought about great improvements in analytical methods; he believed strongly in teaching chemistry through a practical approach and also that investment in chemical research would be handsomely rewarded by progress in agriculture, medicine and various industries.

Such ideas were becoming well known in England, partly from translations of his books, but also as a consequence of the extensive tour of England that Liebig undertook in 1842. In the following year, two of Liebig's former students, John Gardner and John Lloyd Bullock, put together proposals to establish an English school of practical chemistry, akin to that of Liebig's in Giessen. This was to be funded mainly

August Wilhelm Hofmann, c.1855

The Oxford Street frontage of theRoyal College of Chemistry (1846-1872). The site is now occupied by a shoe shop.

by private subscription - probably by landowners and industrialists.

On 29 July 1845, a public meeting was held in London at which a Council and Secretary were elected for the proposed College of Chemistry, and at which financial support from subscribers was promised.

Liebig was asked to suggest a candidate to head the new College and, after various interactions, Hofmann was recommended. But there was an impediment. In the meantime, Hofmann had not only progressed through his formal chemical education, but had completed his doctorate dissertation (a study of coal tar components) and been appointed to a teaching post in the University of Bonn. As College secretary, John Gardner was dispatched to Bonn and, through the mediation of Sir James Clark and Prince Albert, two years leave of absence was arranged for Hofmann to undertake the daunting task of establishing the College in London.

Hofmann in London

Gardner and Bullock took two apartments in George Street in the West End, which were hastily fitted out as temporary laboratories. A grand Georgian house was leased in nearby Hanover Square to accommodate both the College Office and the Professor of Chemistry. In the back kitchen of the house, chemical reagents were made up for the first intake of students and, in October 1845, teaching began in the makeshift George Street laboratories. This intake included many talented students of high artistic and technical calibre, such as Charles Mansfield, Edward C. Nicholson, Frederick Field, George Maule, Robert Galloway, Charles Bloxam, Thomas Rowney, etc. - names that were to be much commemorated in the years to come. Hofmann proved to have boundless energy and an ability not only to explain technical matters clearly, but also to inspire enthusiasm and loyalty in his protegés. Though he had a formidable task ahead, Hofmann had some very willing and experienced helpers at hand - Herman Bliebtreu from Germany, Frederick Abel from the Polytechnic Institution, James Muspratt from Lancashire, as well as his former colleagues, Bullock, Gardner and Blythe from earlier Giessen days.

Hofmann's duties at the College grew to include internal and public lecturing, laboratory instruction, the supervision of research, and the provision of analytical services to subscribers. An increasing burden was the time he was spending on administrative matters - particularly Council meetings, the preparation of reports, and the troublesome task of arriving at satisfactory plans for the proposed College building. The latter was to be erected on a site at the back of the Hanover Square house, and was to have a frontage on Oxford Street. Liebig was consulted on the plans and finally, on 16 June 1846, Prince Albert conducted the ceremony of laying the foundation stone of the College. During that summer, while the building work proceeded apace, Hofmann returned to Darmstadt, and married Helene Moldenhauer.

As Hofmann was later to state, "With the completion of the laboratories, the difficulties of the College commenced".[2] The trouble was that the expected funding for the College was not forthcoming. These 'hungry forties' years were subject to much political unrest and to national and local financial crises. The effect was that the design of the College had to be curtailed, and there was inadequate money to equip the laboratories, to pay assistants or to carry out the analytical services expected by subscribers. Hofmann even gave up his accommodation at the Hanover Square property and set up home in a much more modest house in Albany Street. (This has since been demolished but similar houses remain.)

Under the circumstances, it is hard to be sure why Hofmann extended his leave of absence from Bonn. But it was gratifying how enthusiastically his lectures were received. It was also very gratifying that his students and research had made such excellent progress. Many of his most able students had learned to carry out original laboratory investigations, and to present their findings in publications or at scientific meetings. For example, analytical results had been presented on samples of mineral and river waters, on coal tar products, and on a wide variety of other substances of animal, mineral and vegetable origin. Hofmann was particularly pleased by the progress of his own research on volatile bases. Analyses of these materials were beginning to clarify the molecular constitution of these puzzling substances. He was also glad of the way he had been accepted into the highest echelons of British society. This was undoubtedly due to his warm friendship with Prince Albert and associates like Sir James Clark and Lord Ashburton. Indeed, the Prince Consort had involved Hofmann in what was the most promising development of the time - the Great Exhibition of 1851. The latter had stemmed from initiatives of Prince Albert, and was to prove a stimulus to lift the British

This terrace in Albany Street, Regent's Park, was the home of the Hofmann family from c1847-53. It was here that Hofmann's first child, James, was born. (Their house was No. 26, but later renumbered and demolished.)

No. 9 Fitzroy Square was the Hofmann family home from 1854-65.

economy out of depression into the expansive boom of the next few years.

But in contrast to these encouragements, all was not well in Hofmann's life. His wife, Helene, was ailing with a respiratory complaint. She found London's fogs unbearable and returned to Darmstadt. Hofmann spent Christmas 1851 there with her, but afterwards had to return to London to meet his College commitments. Directly on return to his Albany Street home, Hofmann wrote a tender letter to his sick wife. Barely had he dispatched it when he had word that Helene's condition had deteriorated. Hofmann set out again by train, ferry and diligence - only to arrive in Darmstadt four hours after her death.

By 1853 it was recognised that the funding for the College was inadequate, and so it was arranged to assimilate the College into the organisation of the Government School of Mines. In the autumn of that same year, a young man of fifteen came, accompanied by his father, to an interview with Hofmann, with a view to entering the College. Three years later this youngster, William Henry Perkin, was to make a discovery that was to change not only the direction of Hofmann's research, thinking and attitudes, but was also to found a new industry. [3,4]

Edward Brooke in the ceremonial livery of the Sheriff of London and Middlesex, 1871.

In 1854 Hofmann moved to a grander address, 9 Fitzroy Square, and this was the family home until he returned to Germany in 1865. He entertained many distinguished scientists in this house, but it was also here that he must have witnessed the suffering and decline of his second wife and child.

Edward Brooke, agent and entrepreneur.

The subject of the second part of this story, Edward Brooke, was somewhat younger than Hofmann. He was born in Manchester, one of several sons of a corn merchant of that city. He was brought up in a business environment and, before the age of 21, he was involved in Lancashire and Yorkshire partnerships concerned with refining and marketing the dyestuff indigo. His father died in 1859, leaving him money, and in the same year he married the daughter of a stockbroker. As his family grew, they moved to dwellings of increasing grandeur - from Greenhays, Manchester, to Timperley, Cheshire. Brooke was a handsome, well-dressed man and made it his business to learn all there was to know about dyestuffs, and how to rise in society. He came to hear about the new synthetic, aniline-derived dyestuffs discovered and developed first by W.H. Perkin, and then by another of Hofmann's students - E.C. Nicholson.

Brooke became a marketing agent for Simpson, Maule and Nicholson's attractive range of aniline dyestuffs - an entirely new family of dyes, developed in a co-operative venture between Hofmann at the College, and Nicholson at his London Dyeworks.[5] The Brookes then moved into a yet larger house at Altrincham, Cheshire.

The Caen Wood Towers mansion Brooke built in Highgate in 1871 (see also page 20).

In 1868, Nicholson and his colleagues let it be known that their business was up for sale and Brooke became the senior partner in the new company of Brooke, Simpson and Spiller. Two years later Brooke acquired an exceedingly desirable Highgate estate and began building there the lavish mansion of Caen Wood Towers (later Athlone House). He also joined the exclusive Carlton Club, engaged an agent to work out his pedigree, took to hunting and shooting in North Wales, and had his portrait painted in the livery of the Sheriff of London and Middlesex.

Almost unbelievably, barely three years later, Brooke's partnership paid a very substantial sum to purchase the other pioneering London dyeworks company - Perkin and Sons of Greenford Green. But this was a much less successful takeover. Brooke and his partners had been so impressed by the profits the Perkins had made in the preceding years, that they insufficiently considered associated technical matters. Furthermore, this purchase coincided with the onset of the 'long Victorian depression'. Within four years, the assets were stripped from what had been the first science-based chemical enterprise in the world.[3]

In the years that followed, employees at the remaining dyeworks site of Brooke, Simpson and Spiller became aware that the senior partners were taking too much out of the company and that insufficient funds were being spent on research and development. Brooke, meanwhile, spent his time planning and building two further mansions, while the company slowly declined towards liquidation.[6]

The above tale illustrates how the thinking and training Hofmann had imparted to his students enabled two of them to take advantage of chance and circumstance, and give Britain an early start in research-based, scientific industry. This extraordinary flowering of British industrial activity undoubtedly owed much to the circumstance of buoyant, expansive economics. Its later decline coincided with the onset of the depression and this led to a phase of asset-stripping together with the withdrawal of funds for personal gain at the cost of research and development.

Signs of the changing fortunes of Hofmann and Brooke during their residence in the district are still to be seen in certain buildings (from Albany Street to Athlone House) surviving in Camden today.

Acknowledgements

I am indebted for assistance to the librarians of the Royal Society of Chemistry and to those of the Local Studies Departments of Camden, Westminster and Tower Hamlets.

Notes

1. This article is based on the author's 1992 lecture to a joint meeting of the Camden History Society and the Hampstead Scientific Society to mark the centenary of the deaths of both Hofmann and Brooke.

2. Hofmann, A.W., *Reports of the Royal College of Chemistry*, London (1845-47).

3. Leaback, D.H., *Chemistry in Britain*, 24 (1988), p787.

4. Leaback, D.H., 'Perkin in the East End of London', *Authentica*, London (1991).

5. Leaback, D.H., *Chemistry in Britain*, 28 (1992), p340.

6. Leaback, D.H., *Chemistry and Industry* (1992), pp385, 873.

Illustrations (except for Caen Wood Towers, 1871), copyright D.H. Leaback.

The former Caen Wood Towers in 1992, now known as Athlone House and housing a geriatric unit (see also page 19).

THE INDUSTRIOUS EDWARD WALFORD

Church Row's cantankerous compiler
by Robin Woolven

In the last quarter of the nineteenth century quite the most popular series on London history and topography was Cassells' *Old and New London*, originally published in monthly parts and bound in six annual volumes from 1872-78. The authors were Camden residents Walter George Thornbury (1828-76), who wrote the first two volumes, and Edward Walford (1823-97), who completed the final four volumes. Thornbury, who was a periodical journalist and art critic, had lived for many years at Furnival's Inn, Holborn, and then at 44 South Hill Park, Hampstead. The industrious Edward Walford, who lived for 28 years at 17 Church Row, Hampstead, was a compiler of standard annual biographical reference books, the editor of several national journals and the author of over eighty books, which ranged from classical textbooks and translations from Greek and Latin to topographic works. The latter included, of course, *Old and New London* and his *Greater London* which today both feature on the shelves of most London reference libraries. Such was the success of Thornbury and Walford's *Old and New London* that revised editions were published in part form and in bound volumes until 1899 and, for modern readers, facsimile editions were produced in paperback as the *Old London* series in the late 1980s.

Edward Walford, a portrait from his Patient Griselda, *published c.1894; he is wearing the Order of St John.*

Early Life

Edward Walford was born in Essex in 1823, the son of the Revd William Walford of Hatfield Peverell. He was educated at Hackney Church of England School and Charterhouse, where he was Captain of the school and where he first showed his academic promise. He won an open scholarship to Balliol College, Oxford, in 1840, and was there at the same time as Matthew Arnold, at the height of the Oxford Movement. Walford did not at this point convert to Rome, but won two annual theological prizes, and, having graduated with a third class degree in 1846, was ordained by Bishop 'Soapy Sam' Wilberforce in 1847. In the same year he gained his M.A. and married Mary Holmes Gray in Clifton. Walford 'never held any preferment or care for souls', but took a job as Assistant Master at Tonbridge School for a year, after which he returned first to Clifton and then to London, where he coached pupils for Oxford entrance and had some theological and classical textbooks published. The Walfords had a daughter, Mary, born in 1851, but the same year Walford's wife died of tuberculosis. Edward had converted to the Roman Catholic faith by the time of his second marriage, in February 1852, to Julia, daughter of the late Admiral Talbot, who had been one of Nelson's captains in the West Indies.

The Walfords in London

Edward and the second Mrs Walford moved to London after their wedding, and lived at 31 Chepstow Place, Kensington (now demolished), where they were blessed with the birth of three daughters. Meanwhile Edward had to find himself a career outside the Established church, so he continued his production of classical and theological textbooks, and took a secretaryship in the City. He also started a career in biographic journalism by producing, in 1855, the first editions of a trio of what became hardy annuals: *Hardwicke's Shilling Baronetage and Knightage*, their *Shilling Peerage* and *Shilling House of Commons*. The Victorian demand for such works of biographical reference was considerable. In 1858 Walford started contributing biographies to Charles Knight's *Cyclopaedia*, and a year later brought out *Hardwicke's Titles of Courtesy Containing an Alphabetical List of All Those Members of Titled Families Whose Names do not Fall Within the Scope of the Peerage, Baronetage or Knightage*, the series constituting what came to be known in status-conscious Victorian society as 'the top ten thousand'. In 1860 the first edition of his *County Families of Great Britain* appeared, and this was republished annually for many years. Such was Walford's reputation and ability that he was called upon to produce a biography of the Prince Consort on Albert's death in 1862, a task which he quickly completed, the 192 page paperback being on the streets within 22 days of Albert's death. He produced similar instant biographies on the deaths of Palmerston in 1865, of Louis Napoleon in 1873 and of Disraeli in 1881. Biographic compilation was not, however, the only string to Walford's bow, as he also moved into periodical journalism as sub-Editor then Editor of *Once a Week* (1859 to 1865), and Editor of the much respected *Gentleman's Magazine* from 1866 to 1868. Walford objected strongly when the proprietor of the latter, Joseph Hatton, decided in 1868 to change the character and direction of the magazine. With the support of *The Times* Walford promptly resigned, and started his own magazine *The Register and Magazine of Biography*, which unfortunately failed within a year.

To Hampstead

While these events were taking place the Walford family moved from Kensington to 17 Church Row, Hampstead, sometime in 1860. More children were born, and by the April 1861 Census we find Edward and his wife Julia (both then aged 38) living with their children Julia (7), Edith (6), Ethel (5), Alice (3), Edward (1) and Philip (9 months), and a domestic staff of three. There is no record of Walford's daughter Mary from his previous marriage, although she outlived her father (as Mrs Colin Campbell Wylie). It is also interesting to note that the 1861 Census was the last time his wife Julia was recorded as living with Walford, although she lived until 1895.

Within months of moving to Hampstead in 1861, Walford had returned to the Church of England, and had resumed his title 'the Reverend'. By now his literary career was established, although he appears to have suffered financially from his years in the Catholic church as he was cut out of his father's will drawn up in 1855, only four years after Edward's conversion to Rome. On their father's death in 1856, Edward got nothing while the other children inherited thousands of pounds. When Edward returned to the Church of England in 1861, he lived only fifty yards from Hampstead parish church in Church Row, where he joined the congregation. He again converted to Rome, however, in 1870, and rejoined the congregation of St Mary's, Holly Place, just a few hundred yards uphill from his Church Row house. He resigned his Holy Orders in 1886.

Church Row, Hampstead, in 1750, a typical illustration by Walter Prior for Old and New London *(see also cover picture)*

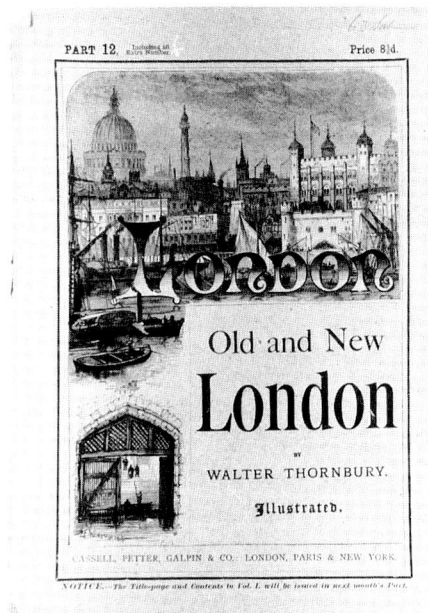

Part issues of Old and New London *by Thornbury (left) and Walford (right), 1870s.*

The Topographic Seventies

Throughout the 1860s Walford had been contributing topographic articles (travel writing with a large dash of local history) to *The Times* and other leading papers and periodicals. Those about London, written under the nom de plume 'Londoniana', were published in two volumes in 1879 entitled, naturally, *Londoniana*. One article in particular is of local interest: originally published in 1871, it was a very complimentary review of William Howitt's 1869 book *The Northern Heights of London*, and in this article and in his later writings on North London, Walford quoted extensively from Howitt. Walford himself edited Charles Knight's *London* in six volumes, originally in monthly part form from 1874-6. However, the market leader in part issue popular publishing was the firm of Cassells & Co., and in the early 1870s they had engaged the author, art critic and journalist Walter George Thornbury to produce monthly parts for a six volume series *Old and New London*. He produced only two of the six volumes before his death in 1876 in the Camberwell Lunatic Asylum. The cause of his death was given out as 'overwork', but the death certificate says 'exhaustion from acute mania'. Cassells thus needed an editor/author to write the final four volumes of the series, and with his experience as 'Londoniana' and his recent edition of Knight's *London*, Edward Walford was an obvious choice.

Old and New London

Looking briefly at the Camden area in *Old and New London*, we find that Volume Five covers 'the Western and Northern Suburbs', i.e. that sweep from Belgravia through Kensington, Camden Town, Hampstead and Highgate to Stratford. Of the forty seven chapters in the volume, five are devoted to Hampstead (66 pages and 22 illustrations), and it is an interesting and easy read, not too deep, and with a blend of the old and the new. *Old and New London* was really 'popular topography' with plenty of illustrations: a pair every three double pages. Late 20th century vandals tend to buy a volume and destroy it for the pictures, which they tint and frame for the public. One of the illustrations (p.22) is a view of Church Row looking West (dated 1750 but executed in 1850), drawn by W.H. Prior, who was responsible for most of the illustrations. It is interesting to compare it with a recent photograph (p.24). The view of the north side of Church Row (see cover) was obviously drawn from Walford's house, and, in a letter in the 1897 volume of *Notes and Queries*, Walford recalled W.H. Prior drawing the scene from the dining room of number 17. Walford's *Old and New London* text was in the nature of a conducted lecture tour through an area, with an emphasis on the old and reference to the new where appropriate, all blended with plenty of quotations from such authors as Howitt, Lysons, Thorne and Park. In his 1968 book *Historians of London* Stanley Rubenstein's assessment of Walford was that 'for light bedside reading these books are admirable; they were obviously produced for the beginner who did not want his text cluttered with learned references'. *Old and New London* was completed in 1878 and reissued in monthly part form at 6d or 7½d a monthly part and bound annually in volumes from 1879-85, 1887-93 and in a 'popular edition' in 1897-98. Each issue updated on the 'new' aspects of London, such as new buildings and the latest census statistics. Such was the commercial success of *Old and New London* that Walford wrote for Cassells his two volume *Greater London* in 1882-3, reissued in 1885-87 and 1893-95. This has also been recently reproduced in facsimile as *Village London*.

The Antiquarian Eighties

The early 1880s saw Walford consolidating his editorial skills on the topographical front, as he had his own edition of Walter Thornbury's *Haunted London* published in 1880 (the theme being London haunted by its past), and his edition of Brayley's *Topographical History of Surrey* published in 1878-82. He wrote several smaller topographical works, such as his Guides to Berkshire and to Essex, both published in 1882. The 1880s, however, saw him returning to his first love: antiquarian studies. Walford became the first editor of a new journal *The Antiquary*, but he was soon engaged in an acrimonious dispute with his proprietor, the publisher Elliot Stock. Walford publicly complained that he was being grossly underpaid for his editorial duties, and he left to found his own *Antiquarian Magazine and Bibliograph* in January 1882. As he explained, writing from 17 Church Row, in the preface to his new magazine '.... to my great regret I was obliged to sever my connections [with *The Antiquary*] for reasons which are well known to my friends and to many of the public.' So strongly did Walford feel about his treatment by Stock, who claimed that he first thought of and founded *The Antiquary*, that Walford privately published his own four page letter, entitled *Author v. Publisher*, giving his side. He explained that he had casually mentioned the idea to Stock who had taken over the idea, but had provided insufficient cash to pay the contributors and Walford, the editor. Walford said that Stock had asked him to obtain suitable contributors: '.... It so happened that as Editor of the *Gentleman's Magazine* and *Once a Week*, and through my Oxford friends and personal connections I was able to promise cooperation, for the most part unpaid, of a large host of good writers, amongst whom were a number of Reverend gentlemen and Mr G. Gilbert Scott.' Stock replied in print, saying that he had offered to double Walford's salary, but that his editor had declined and had thus dismissed himself.

Church Row today from roughly the same viewpoint as that shown on p22

Walford responded by publishing a nineteen page booklet attacking Stock. The affair faded, and Elliot Stock prospered and remained the publisher for Walford's cousin, Cornelius Walford, who himself lived with his large library in the double house that is now 2-4 Belsize Grove (then numbered 86 Belsize Park Gardens). But the Stock affair rankled with Edward Walford, who included several anti-Stock verses when he published his collected poems in 1894. The G. Gilbert Scott mentioned as a contributor was George (1839-97), the son of the famous Sir George, who lived with his family at 26 Church Row. He and his wife converted to Rome in 1880, and were members of the Holly Place congregation (see *Camden History Review* No. 7).

The first of two examples of Walford's view of Stock is from *Ellicott Skinflint*:

'.....But Skinflint the simplest of patents had taken
For a far better thing than just "saving his bacon";
Hard bargains he'd drive with poor authors. His thrift
Was simply to use them, then turn them adrift.
He would suck out their brains and would work them until
He had made them go round like a horse in a mill;

Nay, he'd grudge his poor authors ink, paper and quills,
And he'd huckster poor printers, and cut down their bills;
"Authors' proofs" and "corrections", and costs of that kind,
He would strike out as luxuries "not to his mind".

The second example is from *Authors and Publishers*:
'"That jurymen may live, let wretches hang,"
Wrote Pope. Away with all such stupid slang!
Henceforth, - thank Stock - read we the latter line,
"Let authors starve that publishers may dine"!'

Active Retirement
Edward Walford moved from 17 Church Row in 1886 to 7 Hyde Park Mansions, then a large modern flat on the (now 'Old') Marylebone Road, close to the Edgware Road. He had retired from his journalistic duties by 1886, though he continued to write the legal obituaries for *The Times* until 1891, a task that he had carried out since 1858. Walford maintained his frequent contributions to such journals as *Notes and Queries* until the month of his death, and he also kept up his biographic work, editing *Lodge's Peerage* from 1861 to 1889, and bringing out his eight volume *Windsor Peerage* between 1890 and 1897. But his health was failing, and towards the end of 1891 he retired to 6 Boniface Road, Ventnor, in the Isle of Wight. A few months later *The Times* Court Circular of 8 July 1892 noted 'We are glad to state that Mr Edward Walford who has for some time been in failing health and has recently undergone a serious and painful operation, is now better. It is hoped that Mr Walford, though in his seventieth year, may recover sufficiently to enjoy in his retirement at Ventnor the well earned Civil List Pension of £100 a year which has just been awarded him by the Government for his literary work'.

Walford lived at Ventnor for six years, and in 1894 had his collected verse published under the title *Patient Griselda and Other Poems*, the work of the title being his long poem of 1873, which had achieved some acclaim and was later adapted for the stage. The publisher William Longman told Walford that the poem had made him weep. Nevertheless, Walford allowed himself some autobiographical reflections when he opened his preface: 'I have lived to over seventy without giving way to the vice of smoking and why cannot I be contented to abstain to my very end from the vice of verse making? I learned first at my mother's knee and subsequently at the Charterhouse and above all within the walls of Balliol College, Oxford, to which I owe any good that might be within me and any success I have achieved in my life. Warned by a long and all but fatal illness, I am conscious that my end cannot be far off'. In fact his health held for another three years, and he died, in a nursing home in Ventnor, of 'a cerebral effusion' on 20 November 1897, aged 74. His will, drawn up in 1896, distributed his wordly goods (including 'my house in Hampstead') to his surviving children, to his old college and to friends. Although the *Dictionary of National Biography* states that he returned to the Church of England shortly before his death, Walford's grave is in the Roman Catholic area of Ventnor Cemetery.

In an attempt to complete the portrait of this Gladstonian Liberal, who wrote, compiled or edited over 80 books on topographical, antiquarian and classical subjects, it should also be recorded that he was kind to animals. Walford supported the campaign (not least by publishing suitable poems) to improve the lot of donkeys used for transport in Ventnor, and he left money in his will for the care of his domestic pets as well as for a new suit of clothes for each of his servants.

Edward Walford was obviously an industrious Victorian compiler, but why should we include 'cantankerous' in the title of this article? This comment came from the copy of his *Patient Griselda* at the Swiss Cottage Library, originally that of E.E. Newton, the *Ham and High* local history correspondent around the turn of this century. Newton noted inside the front cover 'part author of *Old and New London*. Lived in Church Row, Hampstead. A very cantankerous sort of man, always quarrelling....'.

THE CAMDEN HISTORY SOCIETY

The Society was formed in 1970, a few years after the amalgamation of the old boroughs of Hampstead, Holborn and St Pancras, to promote interest in the history of the London Borough of Camden. Since then it has had each year monthly lectures and outings and has produced a wide range of publications.

The Society welcomes new members who are interested not only in attending lectures but those who are able to do research at different levels. Enquiries as to membership should be made to the Secretary, c/o Swiss Cottage Library, Avenue Road, NW3.

Camden has a very large local history collection housed at the moment at Swiss Cottage and Holborn libraries, although it is proposed that in 1994 all the archives will be located at Holborn, where better facilities for researchers and school visits will be provided.

The collection includes maps, drawings, prints, rate books, paving board records, newspapers, photographs and paintings. It also includes all back numbers of the *Camden History Review* and of the Society's *Newsletter*, which is published every two months.

NOTES ON NEW CONTRIBUTORS

P.J. Atkins is a lecturer in Geography at Durham University. His research on the historical geography of London began with an interest in food supply in the nineteenth century. More recently he has worked on the West End, its élite residential districts and the street barriers erected to protect them.

Gillian Gear is the company secretary of a family engineering business. Her interest in local history over the past twenty years led her to take first a diploma in local history and subsequently an MA in social and industrial history. She is currently registered at London University's Institute of Education for an M Phil., and her thesis is on certified industrial schools. Her research is likely to continue for some considerable time and she would be grateful to hear from those who have any acquaintance or knowledge of these schools, particularly from anyone who has attended one.

David Honour is from a St Pancras family: his great grandfather was a coachbuilder there in 1883. He is a Post Graduate of the Royal Academy Schools, Piccadilly. He works for the Historic Royal Palaces as Archaeological Recorder and Designer to the Curator. He is responsible for the archaeology of the standing structures at the Tower of London, the Banqueting House, Whitehall, and Kensington Palace State Apartments. The other part of his job is to work on the design of objects and fittings to enhance and expand the interpretation of the Palaces through reconstructed or original designs. Before this he worked for English Heritage, where amongst other projects he reconstructed and illustrated the surviving stucco from Nonsuch Palace.

David H. Leaback, Ph.D., M.Sc., was for many years Senior Lecturer in Biochemistry at the University of London. He has worked in Kiel University, Germany, and Michigan and Columbia Universities in the United States, mainly on super-sensitive methods of analysis and on the origins of science-based industry in the London area. He is now director of Biolink Technology Ltd of Radlett, Herts.

Susan Palmer is Archivist to Sir John Soane's Museum in Lincoln's Inn Fields. After training as an archivist at University College, London, she worked for a number of years at the Greater London Record Office before moving to her present post. She is a member of the Council of the Camden History Society. She is currently engaged in writing up the results of her researches into the history of Lincoln's Inn Fields, a version of which she gave as an illustrated lecture to the Camden History Society in October 1993.

UNIVERSITY COLLEGE, LONDON, AND THE GOWER STREET BAR

by P.J. Atkins

At the end of the eighteenth century the West End of London was well established as the premier district of fashionable residence. Boyle's *Fashionable Court and Country Guide and Town Visiting Directory* in 1800 contained 5,544 names of the élite, the majority of whom lived on the aristocratic estates along Oxford Street, from the Bloomsbury estate of the Duke of Bedford in the east to the Earl of Grosvenor's Mayfair in the west. This formidable concentration of power, privilege and wealth was of course worth defending, and one means devised was the physical blockading of access points. The peace and quiet of the Bedford estate, for instance, was vigorously protected by manned gates open only to residents during daylight hours.

In Gower Street, as may be seen in the illustration, the new University College erected a series of posts and a bar on land purchased in 1825. The original idea seems to have been to regulate access to University College Hospital, with the secondary intention of preventing the establishment of a public right of way across land owned by the College. The bar was at first kept closed but later it was left open all year apart from Ascension Day.

Surveys in the second half of the nineteenth century showed that Londoners were faced with many of these barriers. In 1867, 156 were counted and 249 in 1882. The public reaction was low key at first, but successful campaigns in the 1860s and 1870s to abolish payment on London's turnpike roads and toll bridges encouraged a feeling that other restrictions on free movement should be lifted.

Action by the Metropolitan Board of Works (1855-89) was ineffective and the St Pancras Vestry had to take on the role of agitator for change. In 1879 they hosted a conference of all London's local authorities on the subject of gates and bars. Apart from the Duke of Bedford's estate, a focus of their attention was the bar in Gower Street. After debating the best course of action, they decided to send a delegation to the College Council. The Committee of Management re-

The Bar (seen bottom left) outside University College. From Mighty London *2nd series by W.E. Albutt (c.1854)*

ceived the deputation but gave no hope of removal. They remarked that the loss of the bar would be damaging to both the College and the Hospital.

During the 1880s there was a great deal of political activity by pressure groups on both sides of the debate. Much of the abolitionist protest was initiated by the St Pancras Vestry, with residents' committees proving their most formidable opposition. U.C.L. was involved, sending a letter to the M.B.W. in 1885 when they heard of the possibility that a clause on gates and bars might be included in their Various Powers Bill. The encouraging reply was that the Gower Street bar was exempt because the portion of road on which it stood was not maintained and repaired by the Vestry.

Partly because of the depth of progate feeling, but mainly through the fear of possible claims for compensation, the clause was omitted. The issue persisted, however, and in the late 1880s a private parliamentary bill was considered by the newly elected London County Council. The outcome was the London Streets (Removal of Gates) Act of 1890, which suppressed the gates in Torrington Place, Gordon Street, Upper Woburn Place and Sidmouth Street. These had been selected as test cases because they were in the front line of complaints about access from the Euston Road.

The Hospital Management Committee viewed these developments with alarm. There was 'a strong feeling in the committee and among the Medical Staff that the removal of the bar would be most detrimental to the Hospital unless ample compensation were obtained, to enable them to guard against the noise caused by the opening up of the traffic'. A letter from the Vestry in September 1890 was rebuffed and a resolution passed to refuse further approaches unless a substantial payment was forthcoming. Concern about their own property did not prevent U.C.L. from benefiting from the misfortunes of others, however. When the Bedford Estate was finally forced to remove the Upper Woburn Place gates in October of 1891, the College made an offer. They paid £10 for the gates and lamps, which were then put up in Gower Street as an act of defiance.

Guessing a landowner's price was problematical for local authorities

in the era before compulsory purchase. In 1890 the College had been advised to ask for £10,000 but had not mentioned a specific figure. They were no doubt surprised in December 1891 to be offered £5,000 by the Vestry and a further £10,000 by the L.C.C. in February 1892. The negotiations were brief, with gift horses no doubt uppermost in the College's deliberations, and the offer was accepted in July. The money was banked in January 1893 and, after a mortgage had been raised by the Vestry to pay for the necessary roadworks, Gower Street was declared open on 16th April of that year.

The College authorities had been very astute. Not only had they managed to strike a deal which yielded 50% more compensation than they were expecting, they also avoided the Act which in 1893 abolished a large number of barriers throughout London. The sum total of compensation paid for the 59 obstructions targeted by that Act was £1.

This minor, local dispute in Gower Street had wider implications. In remarkable contrast to the indifference of their forebears, the freedom of traffic movement was dear to the heart of the later Victorians. That the barriers should have survived so long shows the powerful vested interests in the *status quo*. The debate was symbolic of the shifting balance of private and public rights, with the state penetrating ever deeper into everyday life. By the 1890s the intellectual case for abolition seemed indisputable and the Earl of Rosebery spoke for many when he told the L.C.C. that 'he did not believe they could persuade any foreigner who had not seen [the] bars and gates, that they were in actual existence in London in the last decade of the nineteenth century'.

Further Reading
Draper, M., 'Bloomsbury gates and bars: the maintenance of tranquillity on the Bedford Estate', *Camden History Review* 12 (1984).
Atkins, P.J., 'How the West End was won: the struggle to remove street barriers in Victorian London', *Journal of Historical Geography* 19 (1993).
Atkins, P.J., 'Freeing the streets of Victorian London', *History Today* 43 (1993)

Footnote
The author would welcome any information from readers on the life of T.B. Westacott, an activist against street barriers in both the St Pancras Vestry and the London County Council in the 1880s and 1890s.

John Gage
John Gage, Editor of the *Camden History Review* Nos. 12-17, died on 25 May, aged 82. He had been ill for some time after a stroke.
John was brought up a Methodist but went to a Jesuit school - the only good secondary school in the area; he emerged a rigorous agnostic, fascinated by science and history. As he got older his interests covered a much wider span - he did sculpture and drawing at the St Martin's School of Art, he was a good cook and a wine expert, and had a working knowledge of eight languages; he was also a pharmacist and scientist and it was in science that he made his living.

THE STREETS OF WEST HAMPSTEAD

Enjoy a walk around West Hampstead with the most informed book on the area. Where else could you find so near to each other the world's largest collection of modern art, a green telephone box and a medieval brass of a nun's head. Characters include the originator of the gym slip, the discoverer of terylene and the man who shipped the first hippo to the Zoo.

(See opposite for details)